THIS
COOKBOOK BELONGS
TO

cookie Advent
Cookbook

Cookie Advent Cookbook

with
24
festive recipes

Barbara Grunes
and
Virginia Van Vynckt

Photographs by
Annabelle Breakey

Illustrations by
Lindsay Gardner

CHRONICLE BOOKS
SAN FRANCISCO

Library of Congress Cataloging-in-Publication Data available.

ISBN 978-1-4521-5566-1

Manufactured in China

Designed by **Vanessa Dina**
Props from **Judy Goldsmith**
Food styling by **Jeffrey Larsen**
Typesetting by **Frank Brayton**

Hershey is a registered trademark of The Hershey Company.
M&M's is a registered trademark of Mars, Incorporated.
Red Hots is a registered trademark of Ferrara Pan Candy Company.

Chronicle books and gifts are available at special quantity
discounts to corporations, professional associations, literacy
programs, and other organizations. For details and discount
information, please contact our premiums department at
corporatesales@chroniclebooks.com or at 1-800-759-0190.

10 9 8 7 6 5 4 3 2 1

Chronicle Books LLC
680 Second Street
San Francisco, California 94107
www.chroniclebooks.com

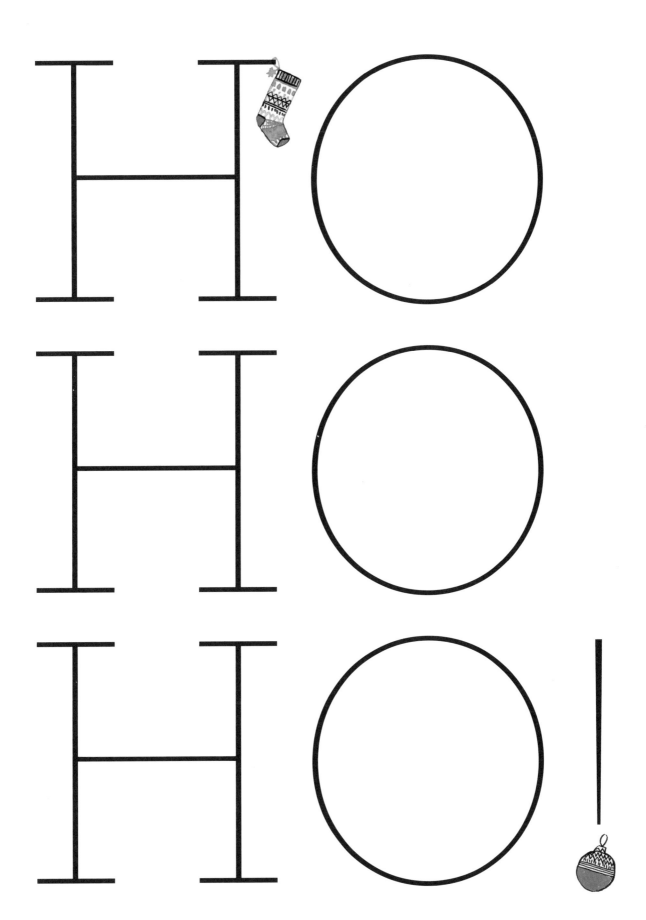

Have Yourself a Very Cookie Christmas **8**

COOKIE BASICS **9**

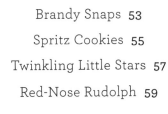

Have Yourself a Very Cokie Christmas

Cookies and Advent calendars are two cherished traditions families celebrate leading into the Christmas season. The cookies are shared with loved ones, and the Advent calendar reveals something new each night leading up to the holiday. Will it be a little story? A cute animal? A piece of chocolate?

Advent is a Christian celebration that technically starts on the fourth Sunday prior to Christmas and ends on December 24—Christmas Eve. Over time, Advent has come to be celebrated starting on December 1; and many families traditionally display a calendar with flaps or doors—one to be opened every day until Christmas Eve. Some calendars last for only one month while others, like this one, can be pulled out and enjoyed anew year after year.

If you love making cookies, this book gives you even more reason to have a holly jolly Christmas. There is a cookie recipe here for every day of Advent. Open each flap on the cover to reveal the cookie of the day that corresponds with a recipe inside.

This collection of favorites includes all the must-have cookies for the Christmas season. Of course there are gingerbread cookies shaped like Rudolph the Red-Nosed Reindeer and cute Cutout Butter Cookies. But you'll also find beloved European classics like spicy Ginger Pfeffernüesse dusted with white pepper, Kolacky with its tangy cream cheese dough and dollops of jam, and adorable pretzel-shaped Kringles. And you'll find a few modern flavors, such as Green Tea Lemon Wafers and Malted Milk Chocolate Cookies, that you'll soon add to your baking repertoire.

Cookie Advent Cookbook gives you a sweet new way to countdown to Christmas with your family, with your friends, with anyone who could use a little extra holiday cheer.

We wish you joy and happiness for Christmas and all year long.

COOKIE BASICS

Here are a few tips and techniques that will make cookie baking a little easier.

Toasting Nuts

Toasting nuts brings out their flavor, so this is a step we definitely recommend. The method is the same no matter what type of nut you are toasting, but you need to watch carefully to avoid burning them.

Preheat the oven to 350°F [180°C] and line a cookie sheet with parchment paper. Spread the nuts in a single layer on the sheet. Toast for 5 to 10 minutes, depending on the size of the nuts. The general rule is that if you can smell the nuts, they are probably ready, and it's better to pull them a little early to avoid burning them. Immediately pour the nuts into a shallow bowl and let cool.

The skin on hazelnuts (filberts) tends to loosen in the heat of the oven. It is not essential to remove the skins, but the nuts will be less bitter if you do. After toasting, wrap the hazelnuts, still warm from the oven, in a clean, dry kitchen towel and rub them vigorously in the towel. Most of the loose skin will flake off. Don't worry about any stubborn bits that you cannot remove.

Melting Chocolate

Any kind of chocolate can be melted, but note that chocolate chips are designed to keep their shape and when melted will produce a thicker liquid. If needed, go ahead and add a little vegetable oil (about 1 tsp per 1 cup [180 g] of chips).

Microwave: Chop or break the chocolate into small pieces and place it in a microwave-safe bowl or glass measuring cup. For dark chocolate, microwave at 80 percent (medium-high) power until the chocolate looks softened and shiny but still lumpy. This can take anywhere from 45 seconds to 2 minutes, depending on the amount of chocolate and your microwave's wattage. Stir the chocolate until it's smooth and liquid. If it's not completely melted, continue to microwave for 10 seconds at a time, stirring between each burst, until it is smooth.

White chocolate, milk chocolate, and German's sweet chocolate burn more easily, so microwave at 50 percent (medium) power until softened and shiny, about 1 minute. If not completely melted, continue to microwave, stirring every 10 seconds, until melted.

Double Boiler: Place the chocolate pieces in the top of a double boiler or a bowl set over a saucepan of simmering water. Make sure the bowl the chocolate is in does not touch the water. Stir until melted and smooth.

Storing Baked Cookies

Most cookies can be stored for several days at room temperature in a tightly covered plastic container or cookie tin. For maximum protection, we like to put wax paper or parchment paper between each layer. Be sure that any iced cookies have completely dried before storing them—you don't want to ruin your gorgeous designs! If any cookies have lost their just-baked goodness, there are a couple of ways to refresh them.

Soft Cookies: For cookies that are meant to be soft, store them with an apple slice in the container. This will help the cookies retain their moisture.

Crisp Cookies: If your cookies have lost their lovely crispiness, about 5 minutes in a 300°F [150°C] oven should bring them back to their crunchy goodness.

Unfortunately, decorated cookies cannot be refreshed. But, in most cases, this won't be an issue—your cookies will be eaten too quickly!

Making Cookies Gluten-Free

There are several cookies in this book that are naturally gluten-free (Double Chocolate Chewies, Mint Meringue Wreaths, and Twinkling Little Stars, for example), but you can make the recipes gluten-free simply by substituting your favorite gluten-free baking mix. There are many commercial mixes available, including those from Cup4Cup, King Arthur, Arrowhead Mills, Bob's Red Mill, and Pamela's Products. You can also make your own, and there are many fine mix recipes to be found online. Just remember that gluten-free baking mixes act a little differently, so you may need to adjust baking times to get the results you want.

A Note About Food Coloring

Several of the recipes in this book call for food coloring for cookie dough or icing to add some holiday cheer. Gel food colorings are a good option, especially for icing, since they won't add extra liquid to your recipe. They also provide a better color payoff than their water-based counterparts, but they can be a little more difficult to find. Look for them in specialty homegoods and crafting stores.

Fun Ways to Decorate

While many of these cookie recipes have specific decorating instructions, there's no limit to the ways to add a little extra to your Christmas treats. Beyond the traditional sprinkles, we've put together a list of our favorite ways to decorate cookies in the holiday spirit.

Red and green M&M's

Seasonal Hershey's Kisses

Red Hots

Starlight mints

Crushed peppermint sticks

Sugar pearls or colorful dragées

Nonpareil chocolates

Edible glitter or luster dust

Finely chopped cranberries

Finely chopped pistachios

Finely chopped red and green maraschino cherries

 Mini marshmallows

Mini chocolate chips

Melted white chocolate for drizzling

Decorating pens, decorator icing, or food coloring painted on with a small brush.

Chocolate-Edged Chocolate Chip Cookies

1¼ cups [175 g] all-purpose flour

½ tsp baking soda

¼ tsp salt

½ cup [110 g] unsalted butter, at room temperature

½ cup [100 g] firmly packed brown sugar

½ cup [100 g] granulated sugar

1 egg

1 tsp vanilla extract

One 12-oz [340-g] package semisweet chocolate chips

½ cup [60 g] chopped walnuts or pecans, preferably toasted (see page 9)

1. Preheat the oven to 375°F [190°C]. Lightly grease two cookie sheets.

2. In a medium bowl, whisk together the flour, baking soda, and salt. Set aside.

3. In a large bowl, with an electric mixer on medium speed, beat together the butter, brown sugar, and granulated sugar until light, 2 to 3 minutes. Beat in the egg, then the vanilla. On low speed, gradually beat in the flour mixture just until mixed. Stir in ¾ cup [135 g] of the chocolate chips and all of the nuts. The dough will be stiff.

4. Drop the dough by rounded teaspoons onto the prepared cookie sheets, spacing them 1½ to 2 inches [4 to 5 cm] apart.

5. Bake in the center of the oven until golden, 10 to 12 minutes. Let cool on the cookie sheets for 2 minutes, then transfer to wire racks to cool completely.

6. When the cookies are cool, place the remaining chocolate chips in a microwave-safe bowl or in the top of a double boiler. Microwave at 80 percent power or heat over (not touching) barely simmering water, stirring occasionally, until melted and smooth. Let cool slightly.

7. Lightly dip the edge of each cookie in the melted chocolate, rotating the cookie to coat the entire edge. Return the cookies to the rack and let stand until the chocolate sets. (If the kitchen is warm, you can refrigerate the cookies for about 10 minutes to set the chocolate.)

8. Store in an airtight container at room temperature for up to 1 week.

Makes about 32 cookies

Stamped Peanut Butter Cookies

1½ cups [210 g] all-purpose flour

½ tsp baking soda

¼ tsp salt

½ cup [110 g] unsalted butter, at room temperature

½ cup [130 g] creamy peanut butter

⅔ cup [130 g] granulated sugar

⅓ cup [65 g] firmly packed light brown sugar

1 egg

½ tsp vanilla extract

1. Preheat the oven to 375°F [190°C]. Lightly grease two cookie sheets.

2. In a medium bowl, whisk together the flour, baking soda, and salt. Set aside.

3. In a large bowl, with an electric mixer on medium speed, beat together the butter, peanut butter, granulated sugar, and brown sugar until light, about 2 minutes. Beat in the egg, then the vanilla. On low speed, gradually beat in the flour mixture just until mixed. The dough will be stiff.

4. Pinch off pieces of the dough and roll between your palms into 1-inch [2.5-cm] balls. Place on the prepared cookie sheets, spacing them about 1½ inches [4 cm] apart. Oil a cookie stamp and press down lightly on a ball to imprint the design. Repeat, oiling the stamp again after every few cookies.

5. Bake in the center of the oven until the edges begin to turn golden, 8 to 10 minutes. Let cool on the cookie sheets for about 1 minute, then transfer to wire racks to cool completely.

6. Store in an airtight container at room temperature for up to 1 week.

Makes about 48 cookies

Ginger Pfeffernüesse

1 cup [200 g] granulated sugar

3 eggs

3 cups [420 g] all-purpose flour

¼ tsp white pepper

1 tsp ground cinnamon or cardamom

¼ cup [30 g] ground almonds

½ cup [75 g] chopped crystallized ginger

Sifted confectioners' sugar for rolling

1. Preheat the oven to 350°F [180°C]. Lightly grease two cookie sheets.

2. In a large bowl, with an electric mixer on high speed, beat together the granulated sugar and eggs until light, 2 to 3 minutes. On low speed, gradually beat in the flour just until mixed. Beat in the pepper, cinnamon, almonds, and ginger until incorporated. The dough will be medium-stiff.

3. Pinch off pieces of the dough and roll between your palms into 1-inch [2.5-cm] balls. Place on the prepared cookie sheets, spacing them about 1½ inches [4 cm] apart.

4. Bake in the center of the oven until firm to the touch but still pale, 12 to 15 minutes. Let cool on the cookie sheets for 2 minutes, roll them in the confectioners' sugar to coat evenly, then transfer to wire racks to cool completely. When the cookies have cooled, roll them again lightly in the sugar.

5. Store in an airtight container at room temperature for up to 1 week.

Makes about 45 cookies

Malted Milk Chocolate Cookies

1 cup [220 g] unsalted butter, at room temperature

½ cup [100 g] sugar

1 egg

1½ tsp vanilla extract

¾ cup [105 g] plain malted milk powder

½ tsp salt

2 cups [280 g] all-purpose flour

8 oz [230 g] milk chocolate, chopped

1 tsp flavorless vegetable oil

1. Preheat the oven to 350°F [180°C]. Have ready two ungreased cookie sheets.

2. In a large bowl, with an electric mixer on medium speed, beat together the butter and sugar until light, 2 to 3 minutes. Beat in the egg and vanilla, and then beat in the malted milk powder and salt. On low speed, gradually beat in the flour just until mixed. The dough will be stiff.

3. Pinch off pieces of the dough and roll between your palms into 1-inch [2.5-cm] balls. Place on the cookie sheets, spacing them about 1½ inches [4 cm] apart.

4. Bake in the center of the oven until set on top when lightly tested with a fingertip and golden on the bottom, 12 to 15 minutes. Let cool on the cookie sheets for 2 minutes, then transfer to wire racks to cool completely.

5. When the cookies are cool, place the chocolate in a microwave-safe bowl or in the top of a double boiler. Microwave at 80 percent power or heat over (not touching) barely simmering water, stirring occasionally, until melted and smooth. Stir in the vegetable oil to create a good coating consistency.

6. Dip the top of each cookie in the melted chocolate, swirling to coat the top completely. Or, use the back of a spoon to spread the melted chocolate over the top of each cookie. Return the cookies to the rack and let stand until the chocolate sets. (If the kitchen is warm, you can refrigerate the cookies for about 10 minutes to set the chocolate.)

7. Store in an airtight container at room temperature for up to 1 week.

Makes about 48 cookies

Double Chocolate Chewies

2 cups [240 g] confectioners' sugar

¾ cup [60 g] unsweetened cocoa powder

¼ tsp salt

4 egg whites

1¼ tsp vanilla extract

1 cup [180 g] white chocolate chips or semisweet chocolate chips

1 cup [120 g] chopped walnuts, pecans, or macadamia nuts, preferably toasted (see page 9)

1. Preheat the oven to 350°F [180°C]. Line two cookie sheets with parchment paper.

2. In a large bowl, sift together the confectioners' sugar, cocoa powder, and salt. With an electric mixer on high speed, beat the egg whites, one at a time, into the sugar mixture, then beat for about 4 minutes, until a soft dough forms. Beat in the vanilla. Stir in the chocolate chips and nuts.

3. Drop the dough by rounded teaspoons onto the prepared cookie sheets, spacing them about 2 inches [5 cm] apart.

4. Bake in the center of the oven until the tops are just firm to the touch and have not begun to color, 10 to 12 minutes. Let cool completely on the cookie sheets.

5. Store in an airtight container at room temperature for up to 1 week.

Makes about 32 cookies

Candy Cane Cookies

1 cup [220 g] unsalted butter, at room temperature

1 cup [120 g] confectioners' sugar

1 egg

1 tsp almond extract

½ tsp salt

2½ cups [350 g] all-purpose flour

½ tsp red food coloring

¾ cup [200 g] white decorating sugar or granulated sugar

1. Preheat the oven to 375°F [190°C]. Have ready two ungreased cookie sheets.

2. In a large bowl, with an electric mixer on medium speed, beat together the butter and confectioners' sugar until light, 2 to 3 minutes. Beat in the egg, almond extract, and salt. On low speed, gradually beat in the flour until a medium-firm dough forms.

3. Divide the dough in half. Beat the red food coloring into half of the dough. Blend until the color is evenly mixed throughout the dough.

4. Pinch off 1 tsp of the red dough and roll between your palms to form a 4-inch [10-cm] rope. Pinch off 1 tsp of the plain dough and form into a 4-inch [10-cm] rope. Press the ropes together at one end and then twist them to resemble a striped cane. Shape one end into a hook. Repeat with the remaining dough. Place on the cookie sheets, spacing them about ½ inch [12 mm] apart.

5. Bake in the center of the oven until just firm when lightly pressed with a fingertip, 8 to 10 minutes. Remove from the oven and sprinkle with the decorating sugar while still hot. Let cool on the cookie sheets for 2 minutes, then transfer to wire racks to cool completely.

6. Store in an airtight container at room temperature for up to 1 week.

Makes about 42 cookies

Mint Meringue Wreaths

6 egg whites, at room temperature

½ tsp cream of tartar

1 cup [200 g] sugar

A few drops green food coloring (optional)

¼ cup [50 g] crushed hard mint candies or ½ tsp mint extract

1. Preheat the oven to 225°F [110°C]. Use a pencil to draw 2½-inch [6-cm] circles on two sheets of parchment paper, about 1 inch [2.5 cm] apart. Place the parchment on two cookie sheets, penciled-side down. Or, line two cookie sheets with aluminum foil, then use a wooden spoon handle or chopstick to impress 2½-inch [6-cm] circles in the foil, about 1 inch [2.5 cm] apart.

2. In a large bowl, with an electric mixer on high speed, beat the egg whites until foamy. Beat in the cream of tartar. With the mixer still on high speed, add the sugar in a slow, steady stream and continue to beat until stiff, glossy peaks form, 2 to 3 minutes. Do not overbeat. Beat in the green food coloring (if using). Fold in the candies with a rubber spatula.

3. Spoon half of the meringue into a pastry bag fitted with a large open star tip. Keep the remaining meringue covered with plastic wrap.

4. Pipe the meringue within the circles on the prepared cookie sheets, creating a wreath design in each circle. Repeat with the remaining meringue to make more wreaths.

5. Bake in the center of the oven until firm and dry, about 1 hour. Turn off the oven, but do not open the oven door. Let the meringues stay in the closed oven until they are dry and crisp, at least 4 hours or up to overnight.

6. Carefully peel the parchment away from the meringues.

7. Store in an airtight container at room temperature for up to 1 week.

Makes about 36 cookies

Cutout Butter Cookies

1 cup [220 g] unsalted butter, at room temperature

1 cup [200 g] granulated sugar

1 egg yolk

1 tsp vanilla extract

¼ tsp salt

2 cups [280 g] all-purpose flour

ROYAL ICING

2 pasteurized egg whites or reconstituted dry egg whites

¼ tsp cream of tartar

2½ cups confectioners' sugar, or as needed

Food coloring in your choice of colors (optional)

Sprinkles, candy, or decorating sugar for sprinkling (see page 11)

1. In a large bowl, with an electric mixer on medium speed, beat together the butter and granulated sugar until light, 2 to 3 minutes. Beat in the egg yolk, then the vanilla and salt. On low speed, gradually beat in the flour just until mixed. The dough should be medium-stiff.

2. Gather the dough into a ball, pat into a thick disk, and wrap in plastic wrap. Refrigerate until firm, at least 1 hour or up to 1 day.

3. Preheat the oven to 350°F [180°C]. Lightly grease two cookie sheets.

4. Place the dough on a lightly floured pastry cloth or board. Roll the dough out to ¼ inch [6 mm] thick. Cut out shapes with your favorite cookie cutters. Using a spatula, transfer the dough to the prepared cookie sheets, spacing them about 1½ inches [4 cm] apart. Gather the scraps, reroll, and cut out more shapes.

5. Bake in the center of the oven until faintly golden, 8 to 10 minutes. Let cool on the cookie sheets for 1 minute, then transfer to wire racks to cool completely.

6. To make the icing: In a bowl, with an electric mixer on medium-high speed, beat together the egg whites and cream of tartar until soft peaks form. Gradually add the confectioners' sugar, beating until a thick, glossy icing forms. On high speed, beat until the icing stands in stiff peaks, 3 to 5 minutes. If the icing is too soft, beat in additional confectioners' sugar, 1 Tbsp at a time. If it is too stiff, beat in water, 1 tsp at a time. If desired, transfer the icing to small bowls and mix in the food coloring.

7. Using an icing spatula or a spoon, frost the cookies however you like and, while the icing is still moist (but not wet), sprinkle with your choice of decorations. For example, we made gingerbread man cutouts, and decorated them very simply, using the icing to attach round red sprinkles as buttons. You can draw designs with the royal icing, or spread it across the entire cookie, and then sprinkle with decorating sugar. Let the icing dry to a smooth finish.

8. Store in an airtight container at room temperature for up to 1 week.

Makes about 30 cookies

Russian Tea Cakes

1 cup [220 g] unsalted butter, at room temperature

½ cup [60 g] confectioners' sugar, plus 1 cup [120 g] sifted

¼ tsp ground cinnamon

¼ tsp salt

2¼ cups [310 g] all-purpose flour

1 cup [120 g] ground walnuts, preferably toasted (see page 9)

1. Preheat the oven to 350°F [180°C]. Have ready two ungreased cookie sheets.

2. In a large bowl, with an electric mixer on medium speed, beat together the butter, ½ cup [60 g] confectioners' sugar, cinnamon, and salt until smooth and creamy, about 2 minutes. On low speed, gradually beat in the flour and then the nuts just until mixed. The dough will be stiff and somewhat crumbly.

3. Pinch off pieces of the dough and roll between your palms into 1-inch [2.5-cm] balls. Place on the cookie sheets, spacing them about 1½ inches [4 cm] apart.

4. Bake in the center of the oven until the tops are set to the touch and the bottoms are lightly golden, about 10 minutes. Let the cookies cool on the cookie sheets until they are still warm but are firm enough to handle without crumbling.

5. Spread the 1 cup [120 g] sifted confectioners' sugar on a plate. Roll the warm cookies in the sugar, coating them evenly. Set on wire racks to cool completely. When the cookies have cooled, roll them again lightly in the sugar.

6. Store in an airtight container at room temperature for up to 1 week.

Makes about 50 cookies

Lemon Iced Cookies

3 cups [420 g] all-purpose flour

½ tsp baking soda

½ tsp salt

½ cup [110 g] unsalted butter, at room temperature

¾ cup [150 g] granulated sugar

1 egg

3 Tbsp fresh lemon juice

LEMON ICING

3 cups [360 g] confectioners' sugar

3 to 4 Tbsp fresh lemon juice

About 34 lemon-flavored jelly beans or yellow decorating sugar for garnish

1. Preheat the oven to 375°F [190°C]. Lightly grease two cookie sheets.

2. In a medium bowl, whisk together the flour, baking soda, and salt. Set aside.

3. In a large bowl, with an electric mixer on medium speed, beat together the butter and granulated sugar until light, about 2 minutes. Beat in the egg and lemon juice. On low speed, gradually beat in the flour mixture just until mixed. The dough should be smooth and slightly stiff.

4. Drop the dough by rounded teaspoons onto the prepared cookie sheets, spacing them about 1½ inches [4 cm] apart. (Or, pinch off pieces of the dough and roll between your palms into 1-inch [2.5-cm] balls.) Lightly flatten each cookie with the bottom of a greased drinking glass.

5. Bake in the center of the oven until firm to the touch and golden brown on the bottom, about 10 minutes. Let cool on the cookie sheets for 2 minutes, then transfer to wire racks to cool completely.

6. To make the icing: Sift the confectioners' sugar into a medium bowl. Whisk in enough of the lemon juice until it is smooth and spreadable.

7. Using an icing spatula, spread a thin layer of the icing over each cookie and top with a jelly bean. Let them stand while the icing dries.

8. Store in an airtight container at room temperature for up to 1 week.

Makes about 34 cookies

Small Black and Whites

4 cups [600 g] cake flour

1½ tsp baking powder

¼ tsp salt

1½ cups [270 g] vegetable shortening

1 cup [200 g] granulated sugar

½ cup [70 g] nonfat dry milk powder

1 tsp light corn syrup

3 eggs

¾ cup [180 ml] water

1¼ tsp vanilla extract

DUAL ICING

2 cups [240 g] confectioners' sugar

1 Tbsp light corn syrup

3 to 4 Tbsp water or milk, or as needed

1 tsp vanilla extract

⅓ cup [25 g] unsweetened cocoa powder

1. Preheat the oven to 350°F [180°C]. Lightly grease two cookie sheets.

2. In a large bowl, whisk together the flour, baking powder, and salt. Set aside.

3. In a large bowl, with an electric mixer on medium speed, beat together the shortening and granulated sugar until light, 2 to 3 minutes. Beat in the dry milk powder and corn syrup. Add the eggs, one at a time, beating well after each addition. On low speed, gradually beat in the flour mixture, then the water and vanilla. The dough will be firm.

4. Pinch off pieces of dough and roll between your palms into 1¼-inch [3.2-cm] balls. Place on the prepared cookie sheets, spacing them about 2 inches [5 cm] apart.

5. Bake in the center of the oven until firm when lightly touched with a fingertip and a toothpick inserted in the center comes out clean, 14 to 16 minutes. Let cool on the cookie sheets for 2 to 3 minutes, then transfer to wire racks to cool completely.

6. To make the icing: Sift the confectioners' sugar into a medium bowl. Add the corn syrup, 2 Tbsp of the water, and the vanilla and beat with an electric mixer on medium speed until smooth and creamy, adding more water, 1 Tbsp at a time, as needed to make a smooth, spreadable icing.

7. Transfer half of the icing to another bowl and stir in the cocoa powder, adding more water, ½ tsp at a time, as needed to thin to the same consistency as the white icing. Cover both icings with plastic wrap until ready to use.

8. Using an icing spatula, spread a thin layer of the white icing over half of the top of each cookie. Let the white icing dry for a few minutes, then spread the chocolate icing over the other half of each cookie. Let them stand until the icing dries.

9. Store in an airtight container at room temperature for up to 1 week.

Makes about 45 cookies

Crinkle Cookies

4 oz [115 g] unsweetened baking chocolate, chopped

4 Tbsp [55 g] unsalted butter, cut into chunks

2 cups [280 g] all-purpose flour

2 cups [400 g] granulated sugar

4 eggs

2 tsp baking powder

¼ tsp ground cinnamon

½ cup [70 g] chopped hazelnuts or walnuts, preferably toasted (see page 9)

1¼ cups [125 g] sifted confectioners' sugar

1. Place the chocolate and butter in a microwave-safe bowl or in the top of a double boiler. Microwave at 80 percent power or heat over (not touching) barely simmering water, stirring occasionally, until melted and smooth. Let cool.

2. In a large bowl, combine the cooled chocolate mixture, 1 cup [140 g] of the flour, the granulated sugar, eggs, baking powder, and cinnamon. With an electric mixer on medium speed, beat until combined, about 2 minutes. On low speed, beat in the remaining 1 cup [140 g] flour, then the nuts. The dough will be soft. Cover the bowl with plastic wrap or aluminum foil and refrigerate for at least 2 hours, or up to 4 hours.

3. Preheat the oven to 350°F [180°C]. Lightly grease two cookie sheets. Spread the confectioners' sugar on a plate.

4. Pinch off pieces of the dough and roll between your palms into 1¼-inch [3.2-cm] balls. Roll the balls in the confectioners' sugar, coating them evenly. Place on the prepared cookie sheets, spacing them about 2 inches [5 cm] apart.

5. Bake in the center of the oven until the tops are just firm when pressed lightly with a fingertip and the surface looks crackled, 12 to 15 minutes. Let cool on the cookie sheets for 2 minutes, then transfer to wire racks to cool completely.

6. Store in an airtight container at room temperature for up to 1 week.

Makes about 42 cookies

Pistachio Cranberry Biscotti

3 cups [420 g] all-purpose flour

2 tsp baking powder

½ tsp salt

1 cup [200 g] sugar

3 eggs

4 Tbsp [55 g] unsalted butter, melted and slightly cooled

1 tsp vanilla extract

½ tsp orange extract

1 cup [120 g] unsalted pistachios, coarsely chopped

1 cup [140 g] dried cranberries, coarsely chopped

1. Preheat the oven to 350°F [180°C]. Line a large cookie sheet with parchment paper or aluminum foil. If using foil, lightly grease it.

2. In a medium bowl, whisk together the flour, baking powder, and salt. Set aside.

3. In a large bowl, with an electric mixer on high speed, beat together the sugar and eggs until pale yellow, about 2 minutes. On medium speed, beat in the butter, vanilla, and orange extract. On low speed, gradually beat in the flour mixture just until mixed. Stir in the pistachios and cranberries. The dough will be medium-stiff.

4. Spoon the dough onto the prepared cookie sheet in two strips, each about 12 inches [30.5 cm] long. With wet or floured fingers, pat each strip into a log about 3 inches [7.5 cm] wide and taller in the center than at the edges. Cover with plastic wrap and refrigerate until firm, about 20 minutes.

5. Bake in the center of the oven until lightly browned and nearly firm to the touch, about 30 minutes. Let cool on the cookie sheet for 30 minutes, then carefully transfer the logs to a cutting board, using the parchment to help lift them.

6. Lower the oven temperature to 325°F [165°C]. Line the cookie sheet with fresh parchment paper or foil.

7. Cut the logs crosswise into ½-inch- [12-mm-] thick slices. Place the slices, with a cut side down, on the prepared cookie sheet, spacing them about ¼ inch [6 mm] apart.

8. Bake in the center of the oven until pale gold, about 20 minutes. Let cool completely on the cookie sheet. The biscotti will crisp as they cool.

9. Store in an airtight container at room temperature for up to 1 week.

Makes about 40 cookies

Kolacky

¾ cup [180 g] cream cheese, at room temperature

1 cup [220 g] unsalted butter, at room temperature

1 Tbsp granulated sugar

2½ cups [350 g] all-purpose flour

¾ cup [225 g] prepared poppy seed, apricot, or prune filling or thick jam of choice

Sifted confectioners' sugar for dusting

1. In a large bowl, with an electric mixer on medium speed, beat together the cream cheese, butter, and granulated sugar until light, about 2 minutes. On low speed, gradually beat in the flour just until mixed. The dough will be soft and sticky.

2. Divide the dough in half. Pat each half into a thick disk and wrap separately in plastic wrap. Refrigerate until firm enough to handle, at least 1 hour or up to 1 day.

3. Preheat the oven to 350°F [180°C]. Lightly grease two cookie sheets.

4. Remove one dough disk from the refrigerator and place on a lightly floured pastry cloth or board. Keep the remaining dough disk refrigerated. Roll out the dough into a square or rectangle ⅛ inch [4 mm] thick. Cut into 2½-inch [6-cm] squares.

5. Place 1 tsp of the filling in the center of each square. Pull two opposite corners of the square into the middle and pinch the edges together to seal. Place on the prepared cookie sheets, spacing them about 1½ inches [4 cm] apart. Repeat with the remaining dough and filling.

6. Bake in the center of the oven until lightly golden, 12 to 15 minutes. Let cool on the cookie sheets for 1 to 2 minutes, then transfer to wire racks. Dust the tops with sifted confectioners' sugar while still warm, then let cool completely.

7. Store in an airtight container at room temperature for up to 1 week.

Makes about 36 cookies

Swedish Thumbprint Cookies

1 cup [220 g] unsalted butter, at room temperature

½ cup [100 g] sugar

2 egg yolks, plus 1 egg white, lightly beaten (optional)

1 tsp vanilla extract

¼ tsp salt

2 cups [280 g] all-purpose flour

½ cup [60 g] finely chopped walnuts or almonds, preferably toasted (see page 9)

⅓ cup [100 g] lingonberry jam or jelly

1. Preheat the oven to 350°F [180°C]. Lightly grease two cookie sheets.

2. In a large bowl, with an electric mixer on medium speed, beat together the butter and sugar until light, about 2 minutes. Beat in the egg yolks, vanilla, and salt. On low speed, gradually beat in the flour until a fairly stiff dough forms. The dough should be pliable but not sticky. (If it is too sticky, refrigerate it for 15 to 30 minutes.)

3. Pinch off pieces of the dough and roll between your palms into 1-inch [2.5-cm] balls. Roll each ball in the egg white (if desired, it helps the nuts to adhere better), then in the nuts, coating evenly. Place on the prepared cookie sheets, spacing them about 1½ inches [4 cm] apart.

4. With your thumb, make an indentation in the center of each cookie. Fill each indentation with about ½ tsp jam.

5. Bake in the center of the oven until golden, about 15 minutes. Let cool on the cookie sheets for 2 minutes, then transfer to wire racks to cool completely.

6. Store in an airtight container at room temperature for up to 1 week.

Makes about 30 cookies

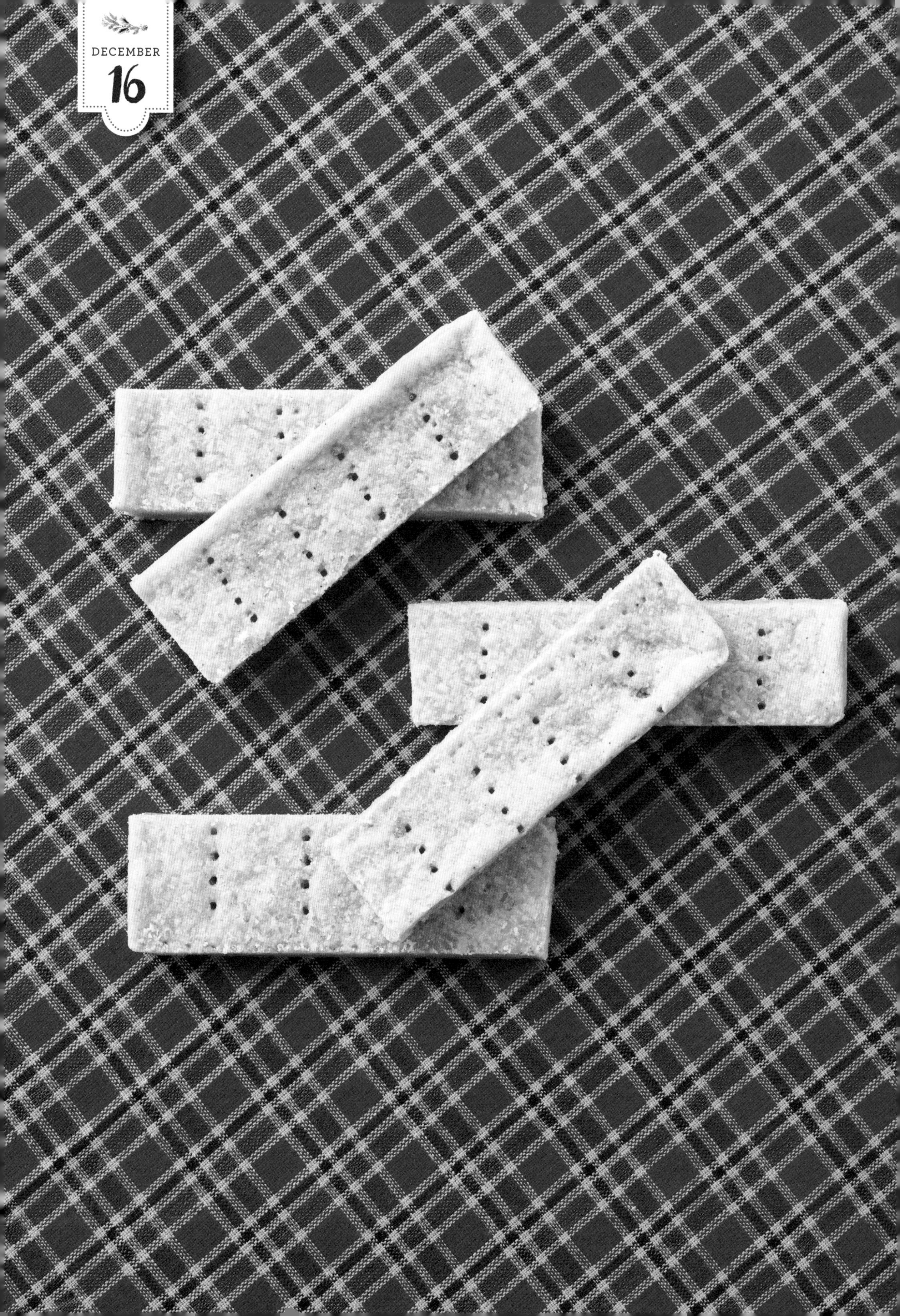

Chinese Five-Spice Shortbread

1 cup [220 g] unsalted butter, at room temperature

½ cup [100 g] firmly packed light brown sugar

1 tsp vanilla extract

2 cups [280 g] all-purpose flour

¾ tsp Chinese five-spice powder

1. Preheat the oven to 325°F [165°C]. Line two 8-inch [20-cm] square baking pans with heavy-duty aluminum foil, letting it slightly over-hang two sides of the pan. (These "handles" will make it easier to lift the shortbread sheet from the pan.) Lightly grease the foil.

2. In a large bowl, with an electric mixer on medium speed, beat together the butter, sugar, and vanilla until smooth and creamy, about 2 minutes. On low speed, gradually beat in the flour and five-spice powder just until mixed. The dough will be stiff.

3. Divide the dough in half. Press each half evenly into the bottom of a prepared pan. Smooth the top with lightly floured hands. Prick the top in several places with a fork. With a small, sharp knife, lightly score each shortbread sheet into eight even pieces, being careful not to cut through the dough completely.

4. Bake on the top rack of the oven until firm and lightly golden, 20 to 25 minutes. Do not allow it to darken. Let cool completely in the pans.

5. Retrace the scored lines in both pans with the knife. Grasp the foil on two sides and lift carefully to remove the shortbread sheet from each pan. Break gently into pieces.

6. Store in an airtight container at room temperature for up to 1 week.

Makes about 16 cookies

Finnish Almond Logs

1 cup [220 g] unsalted butter, at room temperature

½ cup [100 g] sugar, plus 2 Tbsp

1 egg, separated and white lightly beaten

1 tsp almond or vanilla extract, or ½ tsp each

¼ tsp salt

2¼ cups [310 g] all-purpose flour

⅔ cup [80 g] finely chopped natural or blanched almonds

1. Preheat the oven to 350°F [180°C]. Lightly grease two cookie sheets.

2. In a large bowl, with an electric mixer on medium speed, beat together the butter and ½ cup [100 g] sugar until light, about 2 minutes. Beat in the egg yolk, almond extract, and salt. On low speed, gradually beat in the flour just until mixed. The dough should be stiff yet pliable but not sticky. (If it is sticky, refrigerate it for 15 to 30 minutes.)

3. Divide the dough into seven or eight portions. On a lightly floured board or sheet of wax paper, roll each portion into a rope about ⅜ inch [1 cm] in diameter.

4. In a small bowl, stir together the almonds and remaining 2 Tbsp sugar, then sprinkle evenly over a fresh sheet of wax paper or a sheet of aluminum foil.

5. Brush each rope lightly with the beaten egg white, then carefully roll in the almond-sugar mixture to coat evenly. Cut the ropes crosswise into 2-inch [5-cm] pieces. Place on the prepared cookie sheets, spacing them about 1½ inches [4 cm] apart.

6. Bake in the center of the oven until set on top and just beginning to turn golden, 12 to 14 minutes. Let cool on the cookie sheets for 2 minutes, then transfer to wire racks to cool completely.

7. Store in an airtight container at room temperature for up to 1 week.

Makes about 48 cookies

Green Tea Lemon Wafers

½ cup [110 g] unsalted butter

½ cup [100 g] granulated sugar

1 Tbsp honey

1 egg

1 Tbsp green tea powder

⅔ cup [80 g] sifted all-purpose flour

Red decorating sugar for sprinkling (optional)

1. Preheat the oven to 350°F [180°C]. Lightly grease two cookie sheets.

2. In a small saucepan over medium heat, warm the butter, granulated sugar, and honey, stirring occasionally, until the butter is melted. Remove from the heat. Whisk in the egg, then the green tea powder and flour to make a smooth batter.

3. Drop the batter by teaspoons onto the prepared cookie sheets, spacing them about 2 inches [5 cm] apart.

4. Bake in the center of the oven until golden around the edges, 5 to 6 minutes. Let cool on the cookie sheets until they firm up, 3 to 4 minutes, then carefully transfer to wire racks.

5. Sprinkle the warm cookies with the decorating sugar, if desired, then let cool completely. The cookies will crisp as they cool.

6. Store in an airtight container at room temperature for up to 1 week.

Makes about 40 cookies

Scandinavian Stamp Cookies

1 cup [220 g] unsalted butter, at room temperature

½ cup [100 g] sugar

½ tsp almond extract

2 tsp finely grated lemon zest

½ tsp ground cardamom

¼ tsp salt

2 cups [280 g] all-purpose flour

Round colorful sprinkles for decorating (optional)

1. In a large bowl, with an electric mixer on medium speed, beat together the butter and sugar until light, about 2 minutes. Beat in the almond extract, lemon zest, cardamom, and salt. On low speed, gradually beat in the flour just until mixed. The dough will be stiff.

2. Gather the dough into a ball and wrap in plastic wrap. Refrigerate until firm, 30 to 40 minutes.

3. Preheat the oven to 325°F [165°C]. Lightly grease two cookie sheets.

4. Pinch off pieces of the dough and roll between your palms into 1-inch [2.5-cm] balls. Place on the prepared cookie sheets, spacing them about 2 inches [5 cm] apart. Oil a cookie stamp and press down lightly on a ball to imprint the design. Repeat, oiling the stamp again after every few cookies. Decorate the cookies with sprinkles, if desired.

5. Bake in the center of the oven until firm when lightly touched with a fingertip, 12 to 15 minutes. Let cool on the cookie sheets for 2 minutes, then transfer to wire racks to cool completely.

6. Store in an airtight container at room temperature for up to 1 week.

Makes about 40 cookies

Kringles

1¾ cups [245 g] all-purpose flour

½ tsp baking powder

¼ tsp baking soda

½ cup [120 g] sour cream

4 Tbsp [55 g] unsalted butter, at room temperature

½ cup [100 g] granulated sugar

½ tsp anise extract

¼ tsp ground nutmeg

1 egg white, lightly beaten

¼ cup [50 g] white decorating sugar or granulated sugar

1. In a medium bowl, whisk together the flour, baking powder, and baking soda. Set aside.

2. In a large bowl, with an electric mixer on medium speed, beat together the sour cream and butter until smooth, about 1 minute. Beat in the granulated sugar, anise extract, and nutmeg until smooth. On low speed, gradually beat in the flour mixture just until mixed. The dough will be medium-firm.

3. Gather the dough together, shape into a log about 10 inches [25 cm] long, and wrap in plastic wrap. Refrigerate until firm, about 2 hours.

4. Preheat the oven to 350°F [180°C]. Lightly grease two nonstick cookie sheets.

5. Cut the dough into ten equal portions. Roll each portion into a thin rope about 12 inches [30.5 cm] long. Cut each rope into three equal pieces, each 4 inches [10 cm] long. Loop the ends of each piece around each other and then gently press the ends onto the circle, forming a pretzel shape. Place on the prepared cookie sheets, spacing them about 1½ inches [4 cm] apart. Brush lightly with the egg white and sprinkle with the decorating sugar.

6. Bake in the center of the oven until firm to the touch and lightly golden on the bottom, 10 to 12 minutes. Let cool on the cookie sheets for 2 minutes, then transfer to wire racks to cool completely.

7. Store in an airtight container at room temperature for up to 1 week.

Makes about 30 cookies

Brandy Snaps

4 Tbsp [55 g] unsalted butter

1 cup [100 g] firmly packed light brown sugar

¼ cup [60 ml] light corn syrup

½ tsp grated fresh ginger

1 cup [140 g] sifted all-purpose flour

½ tsp brandy

1. Preheat the oven to 350°F [180°C]. Lightly grease a cookie sheet. Have ready a wooden spoon with a long, round handle for shaping the cookies.

2. In a large, heavy saucepan over medium heat, combine the butter, brown sugar, corn syrup, and ginger, stirring occasionally, until the butter and sugar have melted and all the ingredients are combined, about 2 minutes. Remove from the heat and stir in the flour and brandy. The batter will be medium-thick.

3. Spoon a heaping 1 tsp of the batter onto the prepared cookie sheet. Using the back of a spoon, spread the batter into a circle about 3 inches [7.5 cm] in diameter. Repeat, spacing the cookies at least 2 inches [5 cm] apart. Make only four cookies at a time, because they must be hot when they are rolled.

4. Bake in the center of the oven just until the cookies begin to firm up, 12 to 15 minutes. Remove from the oven. Working quickly and using a spatula, lift a cookie from the cookie sheet and wrap it in a spiral around the handle of the wooden spoon. Let cool for 20 seconds, then slide the cookie off the spoon handle onto a wire rack to cool completely. (If the cookies harden too much to remove them from the cookie sheet and shape them, return the cookie sheet to the oven for about 1 minute. They will soften again.) Repeat with the remaining batter, regreasing the cookie sheet as necessary.

5. Store in an airtight container at room temperature for up to 1 week.

Makes about 20 cookies

DECEMBER

22

Spritz Cookies

1 cup [220 g] unsalted butter, at room temperature

¾ cup [150 g] granulated sugar

3 egg yolks

½ tsp vanilla extract

½ tsp almond extract

2 or 3 drops green food coloring (optional)

½ tsp baking powder

2½ cups [350 g] all-purpose flour

Green decorating sugar for sprinkling

Red sprinkles for decorating (optional)

1. Preheat the oven to 350°F [180°C]. Have ready two ungreased cookie sheets.

2. In a large bowl, with an electric mixer on medium speed, beat together the butter and granulated sugar until light, 2 to 3 minutes. Beat in the egg yolks, vanilla, almond extract, food coloring (if using), and baking powder until smooth. On low speed, gradually beat in the flour just until mixed. The dough should be stiff, pliable, and only slightly sticky.

3. Fill a cookie press fitted with a Christmas tree disk with the dough. (You may need to do this in batches.) Press the cookies onto a cookie sheet, spacing them about 1½ inches [4 cm] apart.

4. Sprinkle the cookies lightly with the green sugar. Decorate with the red sprinkles to look like treetop ornaments or berries, if desired.

5. Bake in the center of the oven until dry and set to the touch and just beginning to turn golden around the bottom edges, 10 to 12 minutes. Let cool on the cookie sheets for 2 minutes, then transfer to wire racks to cool completely.

6. Store in an airtight container at room temperature for up to 1 week.

Makes about 65 cookies

Twinkling Little Stars

5 egg whites, at room temperature

⅛ tsp salt

1¼ cups [250 g] granulated sugar

1 tsp clear vanilla extract

½ tsp almond extract

White decorating sugar or granulated sugar for sprinkling

White edible glitter for sprinkling (optional)

1. Preheat the oven to 225°F [110°C]. Line two cookie sheets with aluminum foil or parchment paper.

2. In a large bowl, with an electric mixer on high speed, beat the egg whites and salt until foamy. Gradually beat in the granulated sugar, 2 Tbsp at a time. When all of the sugar has been added, continue beating until the meringue holds stiff, glossy peaks, about 3 minutes. Beat in the vanilla and almond extract just until combined.

3. Spoon the meringue into a pastry bag fitted with a large closed star tip. Pipe cookies just a bit larger than 1 inch [2.5 cm] in diameter onto the prepared cookie sheets, spacing them about 1 inch [2.5 cm] apart. Sprinkle the cookies with the decorating sugar and glitter, if desired.

4. Bake in the center of the oven for 30 minutes. Turn off the oven, but do not open the oven door. Let the meringues stay in the closed oven until they are dry and crisp, at least 4 hours or up to overnight.

5. Carefully peel the foil away from the meringues.

6. Store in an airtight container at room temperature for up to 1 week.

Makes about 50 cookies

Red-Nose Rudolph

5 cups [700 g] all-purpose flour, plus more as needed

1 tsp baking soda

½ tsp salt

1 Tbsp ground ginger

2 tsp ground cinnamon

½ tsp ground allspice or nutmeg

1 cup [220 g] unsalted butter or vegetable shortening, at room temperature

1 cup [200 g] sugar

¾ cup [240 g] unsulfured molasses

1 egg

1 tsp vanilla extract

72 brown M&M's or chocolate chips

18 red candied cherries or drained red maraschino cherries, cut in half

40 to 50 mini pretzel twists

1. In a medium bowl, whisk together the flour, baking soda, salt, ginger, cinnamon, and allspice. Set aside.

2. In a large bowl, with an electric mixer on medium speed, beat together the butter and sugar until light, 2 to 3 minutes. Beat in the molasses, egg, and vanilla. On low speed, gradually beat in the flour mixture just until mixed. The dough will be medium-stiff but sticky. If it is too soft, beat in additional flour, 1 Tbsp at a time.

3. On a lightly floured board, shape the dough into a triangular log about 10 inches [25 cm] long. (The dough may be easier to work with if you chill it for 30 minutes before you shape it.) Cover with plastic wrap and refrigerate until firm, at least several hours or up to overnight.

4. Preheat the oven to 350°F [180°C]. Lightly grease two cookie sheets.

5. Cut the log into slices ¼ inch [6 mm] thick. Place on the prepared cookie sheets, spacing them at least 1½ inches [4 cm] apart. Use your fingers to shape the triangles a bit to resemble reindeer heads, pulling the dough into two knobs on the short side of the triangle to suggest "ears."

6. Set two M&M's on each cookie to make the eyes, and place a cherry half, cut-side down, at the point of each cookie to make a nose. Carefully break the pretzels into antlerlike pieces (not all of them will be the perfect shape), and insert two antlers at the top of each cookie.

7. Bake in the center of the oven until set to the touch but not browned, 8 to 10 minutes. Let cool on the cookie sheets for 2 minutes, then transfer to wire racks to cool completely.

8. Store in an airtight container at room temperature for up to 1 week.

Makes about 36 cookies

Index

MER CHR MS

RY
IST-
I